THE
HARDY BOYS
and Nancy Drew

Daun Showalter

by PEGGY HERZ

SCHOLASTIC BOOK SERVICES

NEW YORK · TORONTO · LONDON · AUCKLAND · SYDNEY · TOKYO.

Copyright ⓒ 1977, 1978 by Scholastic Magazines, Inc. All rights reserved. Published by Scholastic Book Services, a division of Scholastic Magazines, Inc.

12 11 10 9 8 7 6 5 4 3 2 1   10   8 9/7 0 1 2 3/8
                                                            11
Printed in the U.S.A.

Contents

The People Who Don't Exist

It was a dark, spooky night. Wind howled through the trees overhead. Lightning flashed in the distance. It was a perfect setting for a TV mystery.

But who would be out in the dark woods at night? Not many TV detectives, that's for sure! Certainly not Kojak, Columbo, or Starsky and Hutch! They work in bright fancy homes and on busy city streets. What do they know about haunted houses, hidden tunnels, or cemeteries in the fog? Not much! Unlike The Hardy Boys and Nancy Drew, *they* don't crawl around in watery caves.

But it's The Hardy Boys and Nancy Drew who

have captured a big share of the TV audience this season. The young amateur detectives may have to prowl around in the dark to do it, but they have solved some exciting mysteries along the way!

Nancy Drew and Joe and Frank Hardy have been the favorite detectives of millions of readers for many years, but have only recently appeared on the TV screen. They are played on TV by Janet Louise Johnson, Shaun Cassidy, and Parker Stevenson — young performers I have gotten to know quite well.

Although The Hardy Boys and Nancy Drew now have their own show, they are not typical TV detectives. They do not use guns. There are no squealing tires on their shows, no bloody fights in dirty alleys. In fact, we don't even know if there *are* any dirty alleys in River Heights and Bayport, their hometowns. But there are criminals — and plenty of them.

Nancy, Frank, and Joe have been fighting crime for 50 years. The crimes and the criminals have changed over the years, but not these amateur detectives. They have hardly aged at all. Nancy Drew was 16 when she started. Now she is 18. So is Frank Hardy. Joe Hardy is 17.

Where did these popular young detectives come from? Nearly everyone has at some time

2

read stories about them. The Nancy Drew Mystery Stories are written by Carolyn Keene, The Hardy Boys by Franklin W. Dixon. Strangely though, Carolyn Keene and Franklin W. Dixon don't even exist! Or at least if there are people around with these names, they *didn't* write the popular mystery stories!

Puzzling? Perhaps. But there are clues as to how it all happened. The clues take us back in time. . . .

Years ago, a young man working in his parents' store took a brown paper bag from the pile under the counter. He began to write a short story on it. He had been working in the store for several years, but he didn't want to be a clerk. He wanted to be a writer. He called his story "Victor Horton's Idea." When he finished writing it, he copied it over and mailed it off to a magazine called *Golden Days for Boys and Girls*.

He had never sold a story. But he sold this story, and he was overjoyed. He was paid $75 for it. That was a huge amount of money, for the year was 1888. It was all the encouragement the young man needed. He decided he would spend his life writing books for young people.

The man was the son of a German immigrant. His name was Edward Stratemeyer. Few people know his name, but millions and millions have read his books. Nancy Drew, The Hardy Boys — and many other popular characters in juvenile fiction — were born in the fertile imagination of this one man, Edward Stratemeyer.

He was far ahead of his time. He created plots and characters that stunned and delighted readers who were eager for tales of mystery and adventure.

But Edward Stratemeyer was afraid he would be a failure as a writer. He didn't want to disgrace his family if his books didn't sell. So he didn't sign his own name to them. He made up pen names. That way, he reasoned, he could never embarrass himself or his family if he failed.

In 1899, when he started The Rover Boys' series, he asked his mother to suggest a pen name. She came up with the name Arthur M. Winfield. Her reasoning set the pattern for all his future pen names. "Arthur for author," she suggested. "M for the million books you hope to sell. And Winfield because you hope to win in your field."

Win in his field! Little did she know how successful he would become. The Rover Boys were a tremendous hit. Over the years more than five million books were sold. And ideas for other books and other characters were spinning around in Edward Stratemeyer's head.

Soon he couldn't keep up with all his ideas. He couldn't write fast enough. His imagination, once he turned it loose, became a raging torrent. He didn't want to hold it back, but he needed help in harnessing his creative energy.

In 1906, he formed a company called the Stratemeyer Syndicate. If he couldn't write books fast enough, he thought, why not hire other writers to help him out? That's exactly what he did. He gave them the outlines — the plots, the characters, and the settings — and they filled in the details. The system worked well. Stratemeyer picked a different pen name for each series. And the names remained the same no matter who wrote the books.

And the books came pouring out: The Motor Boys, Honey Bunch, Bomba the Jungle Boy, Tom Swift, The Bobbsey Twins, The Dana Girls, Nancy Drew, The Hardy Boys, and on and on. Edward Stratemeyer had wanted to be a writer — and he got his wish many times over.

He always worked very hard. He spent a great deal of time doing research for his books, and he wrote steadily throughout his life. When he died in 1930, his daughter, Harriet Adams, was faced with a difficult decision. Should she try to keep the company going? Would she be able to turn out stories equal to those of her father's? She decided to give it a try.

Today, she and her four partners work out of offices in Maplewood, New Jersey. If it weren't for them, The Hardy Boys and Nancy Drew would never have made it to TV. I went to see them one day last summer.

"Good Mystery and Lots of Action"

I knew that Edward Stratemeyer started writing The Hardy Boys in 1927. He had just begun Nancy Drew when he died in 1930. These books were to become the most popular of all his series.

Why? What is there about these three amateur detectives that has appealed to readers for so many years? Have the same qualities been passed on to their TV counterparts? I asked these questions of Nancy Axelrad, an attractive young woman who is one of the partners in the Stratemeyer Syndicate today.

"Nancy Drew and The Hardy Boys are based on what we call the 'Stratemeyer Formula,' " she replied with a smile. "Edward Stratemeyer used the formula when he wrote The Rover Boys in 1899 — and we've used it successfully ever since. Basically the formula is: 'Good mystery and lots of action, with some educational material.' By educational material we mean accurate information about bats, caves, archaeology — whatever is in our stories.

"We want to get the reader interested in the story from the first page on. So, many times we rewrite the first page 20 times or more. Then in every chapter we have a high point in the middle and a cliff-hanger at the end, so that we draw the reader on from page to page."

The cliff-hangers are usually real beauties: *"Frank, look! The room has no floor!"* Or, *"Joe had disappeared!"* Or, *"The next instant an enormous book was dislodged from an upper shelf and fell directly toward her head!"* Your house has to be on fire — or your mother calling you to dinner — to get you to stop reading at that point!

"Nancy Drew and The Hardy Boys have been updated and revised," Nancy Axelrad explained to me, "but the basic formula is still the same. We think the TV show has been faithful to the spirit of the books. And it has used the same formula.

"Kids are adventurous. They identify so readily with all the things they'd like to do. The world of Nancy Drew and The Hardy Boys is a dream world, basically. Nancy Drew personifies all the best qualities of every girl. She can do everything. She can swim, sew, paint. She travels, she solves mysteries. You name it, she can do it! She is almost Wonder Woman. But there is a human quality about her which makes her accessible to the reader. The same thing is true of The Hardy Boys. They, too, can do everything."

Clearly, part of their appeal is wish fulfillment. How many of us are ever given the chance to solve a mystery? How many of us have famous fathers who call upon us for help when they are working on a puzzling mystery? Nancy Drew's father is the leading attorney in River Heights. The Hardy Boys' father used to be a detective in New York City and is now a famous private investigator. Carson Drew and Fenton Hardy may get paid for their work, but their offspring never do.

"Oh, no," Nancy Axelrad exclaimed. "There's no exchange of money! They are amateur detectives! Nancy Drew has received prizes, awards, trophies, and recognition — but no money. If she's ever gotten money as a reward, she's given it away."

Money — at least their own — is never a fac-

Nancy Drew Mystery Stories

THE HIDDEN STAIRCASE

By
CAROLYN KEENE

Copyright © 1930 By Grosset & Dunlap, Inc.

This was the second book in the long series of books starring Nancy Drew. It was published in 1930. The very first book, also published in 1930, was called *The Secret of the Old Clock*.

NANCY DREW MYSTERY STORIES

The Clue of the Leaning Chimney

CAROLYN
KEENE

Nancy Drew and her friends, Bess and George, don't let anything stop them when they're hot on the trail of a clue. This exciting mystery story was published in 1949.

tor in the Nancy Drew/Hardy Boys' mysteries. They jump on airplanes, stay at fancy yacht clubs, hire outside help, or do whatever else is needed to crack the case they're working on. They don't worry about money unless it's counterfeit, stolen, or enters into their cases in some other way. They live in comfortable, attractive homes. Their lives are quite pleasant, until they get tangled up with criminals who threaten to push them off a cliff or bury them alive in a cave. But they do not depend on shoot-'em-up violence to keep the reader's interest.

"We do not use guns," Nancy Axelrad stressed. "That forces the writers to become more imaginative. It's easy to create tension with violence. It's not so easy to create tension without violence. In the end, it forces a writer to be more creative. One of the scariest Nancy Drew stories is *The Secret of the Old Attic*. In that story, Nancy is tied up and told there is a black widow spider loose in the attic.

"In stories like that, tension is created through the *possibility* that something catastrophic may happen. Nancy or The Hardy Boys are *about* to fall off a cliff or be done in. But they always manage to be rescued at the last minute. Edward Stratemeyer used to say that his books were 'safe and sane.' They still are. They offer good, wholesome adventure and suspense."

"But how can books stay popular for so long?" I asked. "Things change over the years — customs, laws, clothes, cars, expressions. Other popular characters from fiction of the past have gone the way of the horse and buggy. But not Nancy Drew and The Hardy Boys."

"We started revising the books in 1959," Nancy Axelrad explained. "In some cases the stories were cut. In other cases they were completely changed. For example, there was a Hardy Boys' story about a flickering torch. At first it really was about a flickering torch. But we wrote a whole new story. Now it's about a rock group called The Flickering Torch. And on the TV show the flickering torch became the name of a club.

"We try to avoid slang or colloquial expressions that will soon be outdated. Even with the illustrations we try to be careful. Girls' hemlines are constantly going up and down. When we show Nancy, we try not to show the length of her skirt. We put her behind a tree or hide her skirt in some other way.

"We've updated expressions, we've changed train trips to plane trips — things like that. Some of our early books dealt with orphans and adoption. But adoption laws have changed so

THE HARDY BOYS

THE TOWER TREASURE

FRANKLIN W. DIXON

Copyright © 1927 By Grosset & Dunlap, Inc.

This was the first book in The Hardy Boys series. It was written in 1927, and updated in 1959. For more than 50 years, these amateur detectives have been fighting crime.

14

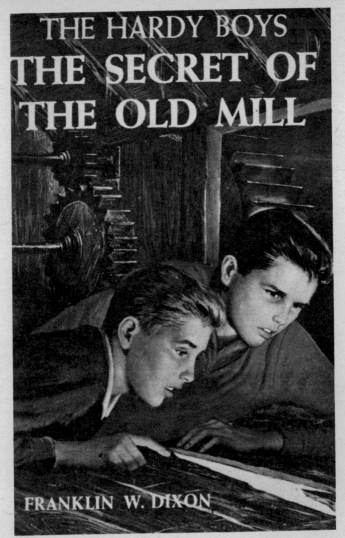

THE HARDY BOYS
THE SECRET OF
THE OLD MILL

FRANKLIN W. DIXON

Peering through a crack in the floorboards of an old mill, Frank and Joe Hardy look for clues in this enduring tale of suspense. It was the third book in the series, first published in 1927.

15

much, that we had to take out a lot of that material. One of The Bobbsey Twins' stories that was written in the 1920's was about Baby May, a baby who was left on the doorstep of a church. We changed that. Now Baby May is an elephant in the circus. It's a completely different story. The generation of readers who read the original story won't mind. They're not interested in the new book."

The Bobbsey Twins first appeared in 1904. Edward Stratemeyer created at least 80 different series, using 150 pen names. And he wrote about 150 of the books himself.

"It's interesting to see which series have survived, isn't it?" Nancy Axelrad said with a smile. "There are now 54 books in the Nancy Drew series, 56 in The Hardy Boys series, and 70 Bobbsey Twins, though about 20 of them are off the market because they are out of date.

"The books we are still doing are Nancy Drew, Dana Girls, The Hardy Boys, The Bobbsey Twins, and a new series called Wynn and Lonny. It's about auto racing. Every year we add one new book to each series. Harriet Adams, Edward Stratemeyer's daughter, writes Nancy Drew and The Dana Girls. I currently do The Bobbsey Twins. We do have outside writers help us on the boys' stories. With the racing series we have someone who races and writes!

"Some of the publishers we have dealt with are no longer in business," Nancy Axelrad said, "so we don't know exactly how many books have been sold over the years. But it's well over 100 million. Nancy Drew has been the biggest seller. She's sold about 60 million. The Hardy Boys have sold about 50 million."

And Edward Stratemeyer was afraid he'd be a failure! That's like the Fonz being afraid he couldn't get a date! Stratemeyer was a one-man fiction factory. One man, hiding behind pen names — widely read and largely unknown!

But anybody who can sell millions and millions of books isn't going to escape attention forever. TV gobbles up material faster than any other medium, so TV producers are always looking for something new and different. Finally, they found something "new" in three young detectives who had been around solving crimes for 50 years. It was time, they thought, to move to the haunted houses. It was time for TV viewers to meet Nancy Drew and The Hardy Boys!

A First for The Hardy Boys and Nancy Drew

The Hardy Boys made their first TV appearance on January 31, 1977. Nancy Drew followed a week later. The timing was good. Cop shows were fading in popularity. TV viewers were getting tired of knife fights and gun battles. TV progammers were looking for shows that would appeal to the whole family.

The idea of a TV series based on the Nancy Drew and Hardy Boys' mysteries seemed a natural. Yet it took two long years to get the series on the air. It also took the determined efforts of two young women who believed in the project — and were too stubborn to give up on it. The women, Joyce Brotman and Arlene Sidaris, are now the producers of the series. They had worked in TV for many years. And both believed that Nancy Drew and The Hardy Boys could be turned into a successful TV series. But they discovered something: Believing is one thing; convincing others is something else.

The story of how they finally got the series on the air offers a revealing look at the television industry today. Edward Stratemeyer had never heard of television when he started writing his books. It hadn't been invented yet. But it's a giant industry today and it almost missed out on Nancy Drew and The Hardy Boys!

Joyce Brotman told the story. "I used to be a fourth grade teacher in Baltimore," she said. "Then I decided I wanted to be a secretary. I ended up working for the president of MGM. I knew nothing about TV then, but I began to learn. Several years later, I decided to get into TV production. I started as a production assistant. Over the course of nine years, I moved from first assistant producer to associate producer. I worked mainly on specials — *The David Frost Show* in New York and a number of shows in Los Angeles. I was learning how to put TV shows together.

"Then one day I met Arlene Sidaris, who had been doing the same thing — learning the television business. We met socially, but we got to talking about our careers. We decided we wanted to take the next step. We wanted to become producers. That was in November of 1974.

"We knew no one would call us to produce their shows, so we began thinking of ideas for shows of our own. We came up with the idea of Nancy Drew and The Hardy Boys. Both of us had grown up with those books. We asked a lawyer to see if we could get the TV rights to the books. He checked with the lawyer for the Stratemeyer Syndicate. Nancy Drew rights were not available at that time, but The Hardy Boys were. We optioned the rights to The Hardy Boys. That means we paid a certain amount of money for the right to try to develop The Hardy Boys into a TV series, and to sell it to a studio or to a network."

Edward Stratemeyer's daughter and her partners back in New Jersey kept a close eye on what was going on. They made it clear to Joyce and Arlene that they would rather skip TV than have their books spoiled in any way.

"They sold us the option," Joyce Brotman said, "because our whole idea was to maintain the wholesomeness of the characters, not to hold them up to ridicule or make hippies out of them. We wanted to maintain the flavor of the books.

We wanted to create a TV series that would be fun and that would appeal to all ages of viewers who wanted adventure, humor, and mystery.

"We had no credentials as producers," Joyce admitted, "though each of us had eight to ten years of TV production experience. When we started this project, some people thought we were two ladies who had come up with the idea while having a manicure or sitting around a swimming pool somewhere! There is still a certain credibility gap in this business where women are concerned. We're hoping to change that for other women."

Joyce believed enough in the project to borrow the money for her share of the option. "I didn't have the money. I was just a working girl with the rent to pay," she said with a smile. "It turned out to be a good investment, but I could have lost it all.

"I mentioned that to my father and he said, 'I'd rather see you lose the money than feel for the rest of your life that you had this chance and didn't take it.' "

Joyce and Arlene bought the option on February 1, 1975. "The show aired exactly two years later," Joyce pointed out. "During those two years we kept asking ourselves, 'Did we do the right thing? Will this project ever get off the ground?" We had many anxious moments wondering if we'd done the right thing in putting out all that money on something that was really a million-to-one shot. But we had confidence!"

Getting the option was just the beginning of their work. Next they had to write up what they wanted to do — and start sending their proposals around to production companies.

"We developed an elaborate presentation," Joyce said. "We worked with a writer and we had an artist do some sketches. We sent this presentation out to various companies to get them interested so that we could then get in to explain our concept of the show. We broke down each of the major characters and described them in detail. We did that so that anyone who was not familiar with the books would understand what we were talking about. At that point we were still just talking about The Hardy Boys.

"One day we discussed the idea with a man at Universal and he liked it. He said he would talk to other people in his company and get back to us. It took FOREVER. We waited and Arlene called him about once a week. She'd say, 'I don't mean to nag, but what's going on?' That started in August. He would say, 'Everything looks good. I'll get back to you.' And finally he did — in October! I was in Las Vegas at the time

22

working on a TV special. Arlene called me there. I was in the editing room working on another show to keep from starving!"

Months passed, however, before the project really got off the ground. Deals had to be worked out and contracts signed. It was a triangle of sorts, involving the two young women, Universal, and the Stratemeyer Syndicate.

"And then one Friday I was in yet another editing room." Joyce laughed. "Universal called and said, 'Can you come in on Monday and start working?' I was finishing an Alan King special. I just turned over the remaining work and left. Monday we started working on The Hardy Boys."

About this same time, the TV option ran out on the Nancy Drew books. The people who held the option had been unable to sell the series. "Universal acquired that option, too," Joyce said, "and asked Arlene and me to work on both The Hardy Boys and Nancy Drew."

It was their dream come true! The three amateur detectives were finally going to make it on to TV. But who was going to play them? The call went out for young performers — and they responded!

"Arlene and I interviewed millions of kids,"

Joyce said in a slight overstatment. "At least it seemed like millions! First we narrowed the list down to those we wanted to screen-test. We found Shaun Cassidy in the very first set of screen tests. He really jumped off the screen. We all felt very strongly that we wanted him. It took a little longer to find Parker Stevenson, Pamela Sue Martin, and then Janet Louise Johnson. We were so lucky to find them all. They are some of the nicest people I've ever worked with — genuinely pleasant, attractive people."

Joyce and Arlene soon learned what it meant to be in charge of a show. It meant a lot of hard work and little sleep! ABC had decided to put the series in as a mid-season replacement. There was only one problem: The show existed on paper, but not on film.

"We started filming the first Hardy Boys' show on January 2nd," Joyce recalled, "and it was aired on January 31st. Nancy Drew aired a week later. We killed ourselves on those shows. What a mad rush! And it didn't let up, because there were shows to do for the week after that and the week after that. For months, we worked seven days a week — and 18 hours a day. The first day of production on The Hardy Boys, Shaun and Parker and all the rest of us worked 23 hours straight! Shaun's mother, who is actress Shirley Jones (the mother in *The Partridge Family*), said earlier that she was happy he was working on TV because the hours were fairly regular! Isn't that funny? On his first day, he worked almost around the clock!

"The first season was hard because we had no *time*. It's not easy to translate books like these into one-hour TV shows. The books have too much action in them to fit into one hour. In some cases we adapted the stories. Sometimes we had new stories written, but it took time to find writers.

"We knew after the first season that the series needed some work. On The Hardy Boys, we wanted to develop the boys' relationships with each other and with their father and aunt. But because our stories take place out of their home, it's hard to do a mystery and then stop to develop relationships. You have to weave that in over a period of time."

On TV there was a big first in the history of Nancy Drew and The Hardy Boys. For the very first time ever they met and worked together on a case! "In 50 years of publishing, that had never happened," Joyce said. "But it happened on the opening show of the fall ('77) season. Harriet Adams, Edward Stratemeyer's daughter, gave us permission to do that. She

TV super-sleuths: Fenton Hardy (played by Edmund Gilbert) is a private investigator who calls on his sons, Frank and Joe, for help on his cases. The Hardy Boys are played on TV by Parker Stevenson (left) and Shaun Cassidy.

had been pleased with the way things were going.

"Arlene and I talk to her and to Nancy Axelrad quite often. We listen to their ideas. They've been turning out these books successfully for many years! They also understand that television has certain requirements. On TV, you cannot introduce too many characters at once. And you cannot have complicated plots and subplots." Joyce paused and smiled. "Harriet Adams is in her 80's and I wish I had her energy! She — and all of them at the Stratemeyer Syndicate — have been very helpful to us."

Could Nancy Drew and The Hardy Boys make it on TV? They could if the cast and crew had anything to do with it. They were giving it their all! The day I met Shaun Cassidy, he looked tired — but eager to talk!

Shaun Cassidy:
Calm About Success

Shaun Cassidy bowled everybody over when he screen-tested for *The Hardy Boys Mysteries*. He was just what they'd been looking for to play Joe Hardy, the younger brother. "He's perfect!" the producers declared. And TV viewers seem to agree! At 19, Shaun is rapidly becoming a major star.

Shaun has seen this happen before. His half brother, David, who is eight years older, became a teen idol in TV's *The Partridge Family*. David took his TV success and spun it off into a rock music career that was brief — but frantic. David was swamped in concert tours around the world. He was in orbit for a time. Then his

music career fizzled like a sparkler on the
Fourth of July. Fame is fickle. David's fans
moved on. David retired to a horse farm.

Now it's Shaun's turn, and his career has
really taken off. Shaun's trying to keep things
cool, but it isn't easy. He had just returned from
a concert tour when I saw him last. "It was
Beatlemania," he declared. "Things like that
are hard to explain. Doing concerts can be very
exciting. You get your adrenalin going. I got
hurt a lot, though, when the crowd got out of
hand. And that can be dangerous for the kids in
the audience too. I've got people protecting me

when I'm up there on the stage, but nobody's protecting the kids.

"I was in a record store in Germany, where they expected about 400 kids to show up. Instead, 1500 came. They broke the plate-glass window and grabbed me. They pulled my hair and bruised me. It's very strange. When you meet kids alone, they are clams. They don't say anything and wouldn't think of touching you. But an inner thing is released when people are in big mobs. Then they have no inhibitions."

Shaun knows show biz from the inside. He comes from a show business family. As we mentioned earlier, his mother is actress Shirley Jones; his father was actor Jack Cassidy. They were divorced three years ago. In December, 1976, Jack died in an apartment fire. Shaun was very shaken by his father's death. "I never doubted his love," Shaun said. "I regret that he died before he saw me on TV or heard my album."

Shaun grew up in Beverly Hills, California, with his parents and two younger brothers, Patrick, now 15, and Ryan, 11. His half brother, David, lived in New Jersey with his mother, actress Evelyn Ward. "I liked being around adults when I was growing up," Shaun said thoughtfully. "I was eager to learn. I was a listener. When my parents had parties I would sit and listen to their friends talk. I had friends of my own, but I really liked hanging around adults. Most of my own friends were older. It was hard for me the past few years in high school. My friends had all graduated, but I didn't graduate until June, 1976.

"I'm still a teenager, but I don't really feel like one. I have my own apartment now, but I'm not there very often. I'm on the road so much. When I was about 14, I started touring with my mother during the summer. She was doing summer stock productions of musicals. I got small roles in several of them, including *Oliver* and *The Sound of Music*. That gave me a taste for being on the road.

"I've always been very close to my mother. She was so family-oriented, it's hard to understand why she went into show business in the first place. She was not a show business mother.

"I was a senior in high school when I made my first European tour. My parents wanted me to wait until I had finished high school, but I knew what I was getting into. I saw my parents' ups and downs. And seeing David's career was a great experience for me. Now I can treat this whole thing as a business, because that's what it is. My mother let me go on the European tour because she knew how badly I wanted to do it. I was so eager to sing and play. I had a band in high school; we played for dances and parties."

Shaun paused and smiled. We were sitting in his agent's office in Beverly Hills. Photographs of his parents, and of David and Shaun were hanging on all the walls. This was really a "family affair"!

"When my mother realized I was serious about a career," Shaun told me, "she said, 'Okay, if you want to go into show business, I'll help you as much as I can to do it right.' That's when she started taking me on tour with her.

"I didn't take part in high school activities very much," Shaun said. "I was so busy with my band and my acting. I couldn't stand things like football games. My mother was always telling me, 'You have time to be an adult.' But what could I do? That's the way I was. People always said I missed out on my childhood, but I didn't at all. I enjoyed myself."

Joe Hardy would certainly agree with Shaun. Joe is only 17, after all, but he's always off solving one crime or another with his older brother, Frank.

"The minute I stop enjoying my work," Shaun said, "I won't do it any longer. Success doesn't last forever. Why not enjoy it while it lasts?

"I did some acting in school plays," he added. I

also played guitar and piano. I was hesitant about doing a TV series when I first heard about it. I had read some of The Hardy Boys books — and some of the Tom Swift books. I told my agent, 'I'm a singer, not an actor.' I've been singing for as long as I can remember. And my music career was going very well in Europe.

"I was also worried that I would be labeled a 'TV performer.' But *The Hardy Boys* is a really good vehicle for me. There aren't many shows where someone my age can star.

"I went through a strange period after *The Hardy Boys* first came on the air," Shaun admitted. "It's scary to think you're going into millions of living rooms! Also, the show is very physically tiring. We do a lot of running. I'm knocked out at the end of the day. We put in *long* hours and a lot of night hours. Often we work from seven o'clock in the morning until seven o'clock at night. I've sung in several of the shows, but I think the singing should be kept at a minimum. We don't want it to be a musical show."

Shaun was unknown in the United States when he got the role in *The Hardy Boys*. His musical career had been limited to European appearances and releases. "No one knew me here," Shaun said. "I had not released any records here. This is the hardest record market in the world to break. There are 400 new singles released every week. A disc jockey plays one or two of them a week. Then it's a new week and another 400 singles come out! You've got to figure a disc jockey will put on a new Elton John release or one like that instead of putting on an unknown. It's tough.

"It's easier for an American to be successful in Europe than at home. I had three Top 10 records in Europe before I released any here. My first single was released here in 1977 — 'Da Doo Ron Ron.' It did *very* well. *The Hardy Boys* played a big part in that! TV is the best exposure you can have in the world!

"I hope to do a concert tour in the United States after I'm done with *The Hardy Boys*. I'm putting a band together right now and getting ready to do a new album."

Shaun didn't grow up feeling any sense of competition with his half brother, David. "I think of him as a brother now," he said, "but at the time he seemed more like an older relative. I was only eight when he was 16. It may be more difficult for my brothers now, because I grew up with them.

"My mother was a strong influence. She was much more a mother than a star. At one time she thought she'd be a veterinarian. But she became

Shaun Cassidy was busy with his singing career and wasn't sure he wanted to be in a TV series. But now he's both singing and acting.

an actress and she's starred in plays, movies, and on TV. She was in *The Partridge Family* with David.

"When I was growing up, our home was fairly typical. We lived like a normal family. My mother liked doing TV because she could see the family at night. I think children of show business parents go into show business because they know and like that kind of life.

"Some things are hard. I have no privacy. I like to go places and fall in with the crowd. That's pretty much a thing of the past! I have little free time. And I go through periods when I feel like a dart board. I'm right out there for people to throw things at!"

Shaun grinned. I asked him who had been the most helpful to him in his career. "My manager, Ruth Aarons," he answered quickly. "She's managed my mother's career for 20 years. She helped me long before she became my manager. She could be more objective than my parents could be. She'd tell me what I had to do if I wanted to be in this business.

"I've always been a very conservative person," Shaun told me. "When I was in school, I couldn't understand the wild, crazy kids. I was calm. But I was happy. I did a lot of kid things and I still do. I *love* to go to the beach. And I love pinball! I'm a maniac for that. I find all the new pinball places around. And I go bowling a lot."

Shaun added, "I dated a great deal in high school. Now I don't have time!" He laughed.

Shaun has big plans for the next five years. "I want to make more records," he said eagerly. "I enjoy writing music most of all. I want to write many more songs. I write music and lyrics. Singing and acting come after writing."

Shaun's leading a heady life for a 19-year-old, but he seems to be taking it in stride. "I've met many people in the past year, but you meet them, and don't see them again. I have a group of friends I've known a long time," he said. "Some of them are in show business, but not all of them. I usually don't like to be with people in show business. I'd rather be with other people. I don't like to talk about show business all the time. You can hear all day about who's doing what, who got which role, who's in *Variety* this week. You can become obsessed with your work and the people in it. I don't want that."

In 1977, David Cassidy married actress Kay Lenz. Shaun was his brother's best man. "I was amazed when David called me and said he was getting married in Las Vegas," Shaun laughed. "David *hates* Las Vegas! But he thought that would be a good place to get married. So I went to the wedding and it was great fun. David and Kay have a place in Santa Barbara where they're raising racehorses. We see one another as often as possible."

Shaun had never met Parker Stevenson, his TV brother, before *The Hardy Boys* came along. Since Shaun was the first of the brothers to be selected, he read with a number of the finalists for the part of Frank, the older brother. "I must have read with about 30 guys," Shaun recalled. "Parker was the last one. I didn't know him then, but now we get along *so* well. He is a terrific guy! He's like a brother!"

Parker Stevenson: "Everybody Loves Mysteries!"

Parker Stevenson didn't come roaring up on his motorcycle. But heads turned anyway. "Hi, Frank!" called one group of teenage fans. The handsome young actor waved cheerfully. He was all smiles. And why not?

Parker stars with Shaun Cassidy in *The Hardy Boys' Mysteries*. He plays Frank, the older brother, who is usually at the controls of the boys' motorcycle. Like Shaun, Parker has become a great favorite of young fans everywhere.

"The response to the show has been fantastic!" Parker exclaimed. "Young people really seem to relate to The Hardy Boys!" Parker laughed. He was enjoying every minute of his

TV success. "I'm so happy the show is a hit with kids," he added. "They are our most important audience."

Parker had never starred in a TV series before. He got into acting when he was 15. He is 25 now. "Frank Hardy is supposed to be 18," Parker said. "But on the TV show we don't really spell out the ages of either of the brothers."

Parker was born in Philadelphia. "We moved to Westchester County, outside New York City, when I was in the second grade," he recalled. "I went to school there through the eighth grade. Then I went to a boys' prep school in Boston. I've always been fairly independent. I was very close to my family, but I wanted to go off and meet new people. I liked the school very much. I was into sports — and I was involved in a lot of other things."

He sounded just like a Hardy Boy as he talked about his younger days. The Hardy Boys have *never* been ones to stick close to home. Give them a mystery to solve — and vroom. . . they're off!

Parker wasn't solving mysteries in those days, but he was learning about the world around him. "I did some theater work in school," he remembered with a smile. "We had a drama club. When we put on plays, they brought in girls from nearby schools to perform with us. My school has gone coed now, and admits girls, but we always did have exchanges with girls' schools for some classes, as well as activities and parties."

The summer he was 15, he got a job as a camp counselor. "The job fell through at the last minute," Parker said, "and I had nothing to do for the summer."

The loss of the job may have been the luckiest thing that ever happened to him. Parker's mother is actress Sarah Meade. At that time, she was busy doing TV commercials. And that gave Parker an idea. Why not try doing commercials, too? He went to his mother for advice.

"She suggested that I go in to New York and see an agent," Parker explained. "I did that and then started making the rounds of everybody who was casting commercials. I probably wouldn't have done that," he added thoughtfully, "if it hadn't been for my mother. She was in the business and knew what I should do. I did it, but she told me how to go about it."

Many young performers begin their careers by doing TV commercials. It is a way of breaking into the business. You learn how to work in front of a camera. And other people begin to know who you are. Parker discovered, however, that it wasn't quite as easy as he had hoped.

"I got *one* commercial that first summer," he told me. "Then the next summer, I got five or six. It takes awhile to get going and to get known.

"Doing commercials is exciting, but most of your time is spent just being interviewed. Then you do a commercial and it doesn't run. Only a handful are ever shown on the air. I've heard that you get to do one out of every ten commercials that you audition for — and only one-tenth of those are ever shown. Actually, I think the percentages are worse than that."

Parker smiled and explained how it works. "If a commercial runs on TV or radio, you get paid each time it's on the air. But if it doesn't run, you simply get paid for a day's work, and that's not much. Maybe you'll get paid $150 for the day, but that's not a lot if you only do four commercials a year. Still, I continued to spend summers and vacations doing commercials," Parker said. "But for the last two years of high school I didn't do many plays in school. I was very involved in sports and in other activities and I was into photography all through school."

While making one commercial, Parker met a young woman whose husband worked for Paramount Pictures. "Her husband was doing a movie called *A Separate Peace*," Parker recalled. "She told him about me. That led to a whole series of interviews over a period of about four months. I wanted a part in the movie very much, but I wasn't sure the school would let me do it. I got the part, though, and they let me off for a month in my senior year. Then we filmed the movie in New Hampshire the summer after my senior year."

Parker was not planning on becoming an actor. "I was going to be an architect," he said. He enrolled at Princeton University where he majored in art and architecture. "But by the time I graduated, I had decided that I was not going to be an architect. I wasn't sure what I was going to do," he admitted. "I considered going to graduate school. I was not involved in theater in college, but I commuted to New York to do commercials. I also did two more films.

"I did not commit myself to acting until I got the part in *The Hardy Boys*. Before that, I had been combining work with school. But now I have committed myself to my work. I'm serious about what I'm doing," Parker said.

Parker has an older sister and a younger brother, who is 14. "My dad is an investment adviser in New York," Parker told me. "We have always been a very close family — they all watch me on TV. My father was a little concerned about my work — about my earning money at the age of 15. He was afraid I'd get spoiled and never get a sense of the hard work involved. He also knew that it was a difficult business. I think now he feels that it can be a wonderful life for me — actors have lots of free time. The business is so competitive. The key is getting work. Fortunately, I've always had many other interests to go along with my acting.

"My mother studied acting in New York for many years. She had a very traditional theater background in terms of her study and work," noted the young actor proudly. "She worked in the theater in New York, Dublin, and Paris. In recent years, though, she's done nothing but commercials because she was busy with the family.

"I sat in on an acting class in New York for awhile. It was fantastic! I began to get an idea of how other people work. And now, in a sense, I'm studying by working. It's all a learning experience. When you're doing a TV series, it's a sink-or-swim situation."

Parker laughed when he recalled how he got the part of Frank Hardy. "The producers had seen me in one of my movies," he said. "So in mid-November of 1976, they asked me to fly from New York to Los Angeles to try out for a part in *The Hardy Boys*. Shaun Cassidy was the first one tested; I was the last. I tested with him and I thought I was *terrible*! Sometimes you feel good about something you've done — and sometimes you feel terrible. I felt terrible! I also tested for Nancy Drew's boyfriend. I felt much more comfortable with the work I did on that.

"After I made the screen tests, I went home to New York. A week later they called me and said they wanted to film a brief presentation for the network. So I flew back to California. We spent one day filming the presentation — and then went right into production. It was wild. I thought I was going to California for three days — and I stayed five months! Everything was done so *fast*."

Parker expects the show to get better and better. "There are so many things they can do with the two brothers and their relationship," he pointed out. "There are a lot of good things there. And a lot of strength. The fun comes out of the danger the Hardys get into and how they react to

It took several years for the producers to get The Hardy Boys on TV. Finding Parker Stevenson and Shaun Cassidy to play the two young detectives was a stroke of good luck.

that danger. My favorite show during the first season was the one we filmed in Hawaii. There was the whole thing of surfing — I learned the basics of surfing to do the show. I loved it!"

There were some difficulties at first, Parker said. "The speed with which we had to do the shows was terrific. There wasn't time to do things over. We'd do a scene once or twice and that was it. In the films I'd done, we sometimes did a scene over 20-30 times. In TV you move so quickly. A lot of it is spontaneous.

"I like to have more time. I like being able to prepare and learn. When you're working on TV, there's little time to prepare a performance, and that's very difficult."

Parker had read some of The Hardy Boys books, he said, and reread some of them after he got the part of Frank Hardy. "At first I wasn't sure I wanted to do a TV series," he admitted. "A series can be a long-term commitment. An actor might end up being in a successful series for years. But how could I turn down The Hardy Boys? They have such great potential!"

Parker is a very relaxed, easygoing young man. He's starring in a TV show and he seems to have life made at the moment. I asked him if he had gone through growing pains as a youngster. He thought about the question for a moment, then replied: "I think everyone goes through periods that are difficult. Growing up is hard! I was always a fairly quiet person. I liked being involved with things like school and acting, but basically I kept to myself. When I was in college, I sang with a group that traveled a lot and I rowed crew at Princeton, so I met many people. I dated quite a bit, too," he added.

"I like a girl who is independent and who has activities that she's involved in — no matter what they are, so long as they are things she likes and gets a charge out of doing. I like people who have interests and get excited about things!"

At this point in his life, Parker is excited about many things. "My immediate hopes," he said enthusiastically, "are to continue doing *The Hardy Boys* and maybe some other TV and film work. I'm also reading like crazy to see if I can find projects I like that I might be able to do. I don't want to sit back and wait for people to bring properties to me. I like the idea of finding properties and producing them myself.

"I love seeing movies — and I consider them my homework. I like to see what others are doing. I can't help but take a critical eye into the theater with me when I go to the movies. There is always a little extra awareness when you're in the same business. I watch TV, too, but I prefer to go out. I watch more TV now than I used to because of our series. I have to see what others are doing."

Parker tries to stay active, no matter how busy he gets with his acting. "I exercise regularly," he said. "I try to run every day. I still have an apartment in New York. New York is refreshing. But I like Los Angeles. The weather is great for anyone who loves outdoor sports."

Parker was suddenly reminded of the young fans who greet him wherever he goes. He smiled at the thought. "You know," he pointed out, "The Hardy Boys are very special. They are very all-American. They are clean-cut, adventurous, bright young men. The fact that their father is a detective makes the stories seem realistic. My own brother is much younger than I am, but sometimes I draw on my relationship with him when I'm playing Frank Hardy."

"Are young people today anything like The Hardy Boys?" I asked Parker.

"Of course they are!" he exclaimed. "Maybe their fathers aren't detectives, but kids today are bright and adventurous! Everybody loves mysteries and stealing around looking for clues. We had a haunted house in our first show. That was fun. Boy, did we work long and hard on that show!"

Was it worth it?

"Absolutely!" Parker replied. "We want to do the best show we possibly can, and that takes time."

And the young fans? "They're wonderful!" Parker replied as we parted and he took off down the street. He didn't need Frank Hardy's motorcycle. He was doing just fine on his own two feet!

Vroom . . . The Hardy Boys roar off on another of their adventures. One thing is sure: the TV crime-fighters always catch the bad guys.

Janet Louise Johnson: A New Look for Nancy Drew

Finding the right people to star in a TV series is never easy. A lot of luck is involved. Producers interview dozens of actors and actresses. Then they make their choices—and cross their fingers. Nobody ever knows how a series will develop or whom the audience will like.

The Hardy Boys and Nancy Drew had not been on the air long before one thing became clear. Audiences liked The Hardy Boys. But Nancy Drew—on her own—didn't fare as well. Fewer people tuned in to watch her. The ratings for the shows went up when The Hardy Boys were on and down when it was Nancy Drew's week.

Why was this so? Nobody knows for sure. But

whatever the reasons, something had to be done. The producers decided to combine the two shows. Nancy had already worked with Frank and Joe in a couple of stories. Why not continue to have the three of them working together?

The idea seemed fine to everybody except Pamela Sue Martin, who was then playing Nancy Drew. Pam hated to see Nancy Drew lose her own show, and was not sure she could be happy in a combined show. Finally it was agreed that a new Nancy Drew would be found. Pam would move on to other acting roles.

For the producers of the show, it meant another round of interviewing young actresses. However, their job turned out to be easier than they had expected. One day a teenager with practically no acting experience walked into their office. Her name was Janet Louise Johnson. She was very pretty, very pleasant—and very nervous. "I was scared to death, in fact," Janet recalled.

"They asked me to read part of a script. I was nervous because I hadn't done a reading for several months. I gave what I thought was a *horrible* reading. Then I went home and forgot about it. I thought I had blown it."

But the producers saw beyond the nervousness. They saw a bright, attractive young woman who just might turn out to be their new Nancy Drew. They asked Janet to come back.

"At the end of the week I did a screen test for them," Janet told me. "Studio and network executives looked at it over the weekend. Then they called me on Monday and told me I had the job."

Janet was stunned. "My mother was with me when I got the call," she said. "We didn't know what to do or how to react. We just looked at each other!"

Janet played Nancy Drew in four episodes of *The Hardy Boys* during the winter and spring of 1978. One of those episodes was a real thriller. In it, Nancy was kidnapped and held captive on top of a skyscraper. By the time The Hardy Boys reached her, the building was on fire—and escape seemed impossible. But a little derring-do—including a dangerous climb up an elevator shaft—saved the day. For Janet Louise Johnson, it was quite an introduction to her Nancy Drew role! Nobody ever said playing an amateur detective was dull work!

But who is Janet Louise Johnson when she's not playing Nancy Drew? I asked the young actress about herself and her family. She grew up in North Hollywood, California, she told me. "I lived with my parents and three sisters," she said. "Two of my sisters are older, one is younger. My dad is semi-retired now. He and Mom are working together in real estate."

Janet went to North Hollywood High School. "I graduated in 1976," she said. "I was very interested in acting when I was in school, but the acting group in our school was very 'clubbish.' They all stuck together. I didn't feel I fit in with them. I wanted to act, but I had no confidence in my acting. So I put it out of my mind."

She became a cheerleader instead and was also

Janet Louise Johnson is a very active person. "I don't like to sit around too much," she says. "I like the beach and tennis and swimming in the ocean." She also enjoys skiing.

elected a homecoming princess. "I was a good student in high school," she remembered. "And even though I didn't join the drama group, I had a couple of real small parts in their plays.

"I was always busy. In my senior year, I was getting ready to go to UCLA. I wasn't sure what I wanted to take there, but I liked the school."

Once she got into college, Janet thought that she'd major in theater arts. She tried out some of the courses, but they weren't really what she had in mind. "They were technical courses in costumes and makeup and lighting and so on," she said. "I wanted acting. Finally I asked myself: 'What am I doing here at UCLA?' By that time, I had started doing some fashion modeling for a teenage magazine and I was beginning to go out on interviews for commercials and acting parts. I began to miss a lot of school and that worried me. There wasn't enough time to do everything I wanted to do!"

At the beginning of her sophomore year at UCLA, Janet met the head of a modeling school in New York. "The woman was very nice to me," Janet said. "She told me I could stay with her if I wanted to go to New York. So I quit school and headed there.

"I got a modeling assignment that sent me to New Orleans and to The Bahamas. Then I also got to model clothes on *The Mike Douglas Show*. That was really fun!"

Not long after that, Janet returned home to California. She didn't know it then, but she was also heading for her first real acting job. "Until I got the part of Nancy Drew, I had done very little acting," she admitted. "I had a *really* small part in a movie and I appeared on the *Donny and Marie* show in a short skit. And I had done a couple of TV commercials. That's all."

Janet laughed. She is a friendly, outgoing person who doesn't take herself too seriously. She is delighted to have had the chance to play Nancy Drew. "I don't know how many shows they will use me in," she revealed. "But no matter what happens, I have still learned so much. And everybody involved with the series has been just wonderful. I was not too familiar with the show when I came into it, and I think that was good. I could approach the role in my own way.

"I always loved the Nancy Drew books. I have read almost all of them. And I started taking acting lessons so I can play Nancy Drew better—or any other roles that come along!"

Janet's family, she said, were always very supportive of her. "They encouraged me to do whatever I wanted to do," she noted, "and I think that's very important for a family to do. Being in a TV show was such a huge jump in my career. Having my family behind me through all of this has really meant a lot."

The hardest thing about being in a TV show, the young actress discovered, "was getting used to the rhythm of the work. You spend so much time sitting around waiting, then it's time to do a scene and you have to get your whole energy level up again."

Nonetheless, playing Nancy Drew has convinced Janet that she enjoys acting. "I want to

In one of Janet Louise Johnson's first roles as Nancy Drew, she was rescued from the top of a burning skyscraper by Frank and Joe Hardy. She might return the favor by rescuing them in future episodes.

continue doing it," she said. "I wasn't really sure until I actually got a part to play! After I did the four shows in the spring of 1978, I went to Palm Springs to vacation for a few days, and I found that I didn't really want to vacation. I wanted to work. I don't feel good unless I'm working or doing something to improve myself.

"I don't like to sit around too much," she added.

"I like the beach and tennis and swimming in the ocean. And I work out in the gym three days a week. I have lots of friends, but only three or four really close ones. I go out a lot, too, but I don't have a special boyfriend."

In just a few weeks, Janet managed to bring her own style and grace to the role of Nancy Drew. It is a part she enjoys playing, and she hopes Nancy (and she!) will continue to be of value to The Hardy Boys.

Pamela Sue Martin, who first played Nancy Drew in the TV series, began her career in much the same way as Janet Louise Johnson did. She was a junior in high school when a friend suggested she try modeling in New York. "I didn't like modeling too much," Pam told me, "but gradually I got into doing TV commercials.

"I dropped out of school for part of my senior year to do a film. It was amazing! I had done a couple of commercials, and the people at the agency asked me if I wanted to audition for a film. I auditioned in New York and I got the part. I didn't know anything about making movies! I did the film and then went back to high school in the spring."

When Pamela Sue Martin played Nancy Drew, she enjoyed Nancy's relationship with her father, Carson Drew, a criminal lawyer played by William Schallert.

Pam grew up in Westport, Connecticut, but moved to California about six years ago. She has been in several movies, including *The Poseidon Adventure*. "And I want to do many more feature films," she said.

One thing she especially enjoyed about Nancy Drew was Nancy's relationship with her father. "I can relate to that," she explained. "Nancy is independent and he allows that. He's never condescending. My own father was that way.

"I think one reason kids identify with Nancy Drew is because she is a borderline adult. She's not really an adult yet, but she steps over the line. Sometimes she does things she's not supposed to do—and that's fun."

Pam isn't playing Nancy Drew anymore, but the role was a major boost to her career. It introduced her to millions of TV viewers and gave her a chance to learn what it was like to be an actress and an amateur detective.

Bats in the Lighthouse

Whispering walls . . . blinking lights . . . disappearing statues . . . strange happenings in the night . . .

That is the world of Nancy Drew and The Hardy Boys. There are mysteries to be solved, clues to be followed. And one thing is certain — the young detectives won't be baffled for long. They have been solving crimes for 50 years. They've been chasing bad guys longer than anybody on television.

TV detectives come and go. They are like the blinking light in the haunted house: on-again, off-again. TV viewers get tired of seeing the same people year after year. Columbo and his rumpled raincoat were a novelty. So were Ko-jak and his lollipops, and Baretta and his bird. But the novelty wore off. Each week's episode began to sound like the one the week before.

But for 50 years, Nancy Drew and The Hardy Boys held their audiences. Loyal readers tingled with excitement at their every adventure. Edward Stratemeyer had created them and had laid down the ground rules for their development: good mystery and lots of action.

The books are classic detective stories. They are works of fiction about a puzzling crime, a number of clues, and detectives who solve the mystery. Edward Stratemeyer didn't invent the detective story — Edgar Allan Poe and other writers began writing them in the 1800's. But Stratemeyer was writing for young people. So he built his stories around young detectives and let *them* solve the crimes. Maybe it was their fathers who got them involved in the different cases — but it was always easy enough to send Carson Drew and Fenton Hardy out of town on other business. Somehow, Nancy Drew and The Hardy Boys always managed to save themselves — and solve the crime — just in the nick of time! Then — and only then — could their fathers reappear and congratulate them on the fine job they'd done!

It was a formula that worked over and over and over again. Other writers tried to match it, but none came close.

Even the Stratemeyer Syndicate — the people who write Nancy Drew and The Hardy Boys — tried to come up with different ideas and new characters. But the readers didn't want them. They wanted Nancy Drew and The Hardy Boys!

Why is that? I asked Nancy Axelrad, one of the partners in the Stratemeyer Syndicate. She explained, "It usually takes several years for a new series to catch on. And you can't be sure that it ever will. We came up with the idea for a spy series called Christopher Cool, Teen Spy. There were six books in the series. It was a good series with lots of action, but . . . it's off the market now.

"We simply haven't found anything that can match the popularity of Nancy Drew and The Hardy Boys. Nancy Drew, The Hardy Boys, and The Bobbsey Twins are so well known. They have a built-in audience that has come down through at least three generations of readers. How do you compete with that?"

Christopher Cool couldn't. He turned in his spyglass and retired. The spies were safe — if they stayed away from River Heights or

Bayport. They were in trouble if they got anywhere near those two towns!

Nancy Drew and The Hardy Boys don't operate alone. They have friends who help out. Those friends play an important role in the books. They provide the contrast — and the humor. Chet Morton, Frank and Joe Hardy's friend, is a chunky, round-faced young man who is never quite sure he wants to get involved in the Hardys' adventures. He may be forced into facing danger head-on, but he's always ready to run in the opposite direction.

Nancy Drew has similar friends: plump Bess Marvin and her cousin George Fayne. She describes both girls as "part of my detective force," but they are the followers of the force. Nancy is the leader, the one who puts all the clues together and comes up with the answer to the puzzle. Bess and George help her out, but they aren't the ones who are quick-witted and adept at solving crimes. All of that is left up to Nancy Drew.

Over the years, the characters have been carefully defined. Each one of them serves a purpose. The authors know that young readers will keep coming back for more mystery and adventure — but only if they care about the people involved.

Readers of The Hardy Boys books had their own visual images of Frank and Joe Hardy. Parker Stevenson and Shaun Cassidy did not fit every reader's image, but many TV viewers think they fit the roles perfectly.

All of the characters, however, did not make it into the TV show — at least at first. Bess was eliminated the first season. "And the mail poured in," exclaimed Nancy Axelrad. "Everybody wanted to know, 'Where's Bess?'

"The TV producers had asked us if they could eliminate Bess and we had given our permission. We knew we would get mail! The producers felt that there were too many characters to introduce all at once. TV apparently works better with fewer characters. Our books have more characters and more complicated plots, with a main plot and at least one subplot."

Mail also poured in from young people who didn't think the characters looked quite right. All of us who have read the books have our own ideas of what Nancy Drew and The Hardy Boys look like. Nobody could question us, for we were seeing them in our own imaginations. But seeing them on TV? "Oh, no!" challenged some viewers.

"Much of the mail was about George," Nancy Axelrad revealed. "Young people wrote: 'But George has *short* dark hair!' Jean Rasey, who played George, had beautiful *long* dark hair. She cut it after the first few shows!" Nancy laughed.

"Readers have their own visual images of Nancy, Ned, George, Frank, and Joe Hardy," she continued. "That's one of the beauties of the books. We do not give lengthy descriptions of the people. We want readers to project their own feelings and decide for themselves what the characters look like. Seeing those characters on the TV screen is a different matter. Once you see them on the screen, they're set."

Clearly, books and TV are very different. Reading and watching are two different activities, and the same rules do not apply. The people who write the books know that. Their concern all along has been to keep the spirit of the books in any TV adaptation. Some years ago, they permitted a film company to turn The Hardy Boys into a TV cartoon. They soon discovered they had made a mistake.

"The film company turned the stories into 15-minute cartoons and showed two of them in each half hour show," Nancy recalled. "The stories were so action-packed, you couldn't follow them at all. It was not a success.

"Nancy Drew has never been done in animation, although she did make it into the movies in the 1940's. Nancy Drew has been optioned to various companies through the years, but for one reason or another she never made it onto the TV screen until now. We felt that Universal would maintain the spirit of the books. They assured us they wanted to do a live action show, not a cartoon, that would be true to the characters and the plots of the books. They check everything they do with us. It's been a very happy arrangement."

So happy, in fact, that there's talk now of developing a TV series based on four other books: The Rover Boys, Tom Swift, The Bobbsey Twins, and Bomba the Jungle Boy.

"We're reviving the books of Bomba the Jungle Boy," said Nancy Axelrad. "That's an old series that was written during the 1920's. It's like the old Tarzan stories. It will be very exciting."

The appeal of Nancy Drew and The Hardy Boys has gone far beyond the shores of the United States. Each series has been translated into 14 different languages. Just recently, they were translated into Japanese, Hebrew, and Indonesian.

"Nancy Drew is the top-selling juvenile book in France," Nancy Axelrad revealed proudly. "They don't call her Nancy there, though. They call her Alice — only they pronounce it in a very French way! The publisher in France said Nancy is the name of a rather unsavory seaport, so they changed her name. And in Germany her name is Susanne Langen. There, she is 21 and a lawyer. The publisher there said that no German girl of 18 would be allowed to solve mysteries the way Nancy Drew does."

Would American girls? Nancy Axelrad smiled.

"Nancy Drew is the American dream," she answered. "The series was started in 1930. I think we'd know by now if we should have changed the character. She is an ideal for young American girls. Maybe that's because this is the land of opportunity."

Nancy had told me earlier that there were 54 books in the Nancy Drew series — and even more in The Hardy Boys series. "How do you keep track of what's been written in each series?" I asked her.

"I have a card file on *every* character," she replied. "That card tells where each person lives, who they know, where they've traveled. It tells everything about them. For the Nancy Drew books alone, the file is at least four inches thick. Her hometown, River Heights, is a growing town after all these years! It has a post office, a theater, a taxi company . . . I have a list of all the streets, and so on."

"Where is River Heights?" I wondered.

"I have a feeling it's in Ohio," Nancy responded. "But readers can place it anywhere. You know," she added, "Edward Stratemeyer had such a vivid imagination. He got that into his books and it even extended to his pen names. They were all upbeat: Carolyn Keene for Nancy Drew, Laura Lee Hope for The Bobbsey Twins. The only one I can't really figure out is Franklin W. Dixon, the name he used for The

Hardy Boys. But I bet anything that the W is for Win!"

Edward Stratemeyer always researched his books very carefully. So do the people who are writing them today. Nancy Axelrad learned, however, that the TV production people weren't always interested in her research. They had their own problems!

"I went to Oregon with them when they filmed the first Nancy Drew show," she said. "They were filming at a lighthouse up there. In one scene, Nancy was exploring the interior of the lighthouse and a bat frightened her I had done a great deal of research on bats for another story I'd worked on. So I knew a lot about bats. They had just one bat frightening Nancy. I raised the question: 'Shouldn't there be more than one bat?' I asked the director, and he said: 'Do you know how much that one bat cost? $600!' " Nancy Axelrad laughed. "Sure, I knew bats travel in groups. But he made his point.

"We are so aware of all the little things, though. We research every detail and often travel to do it. We use libraries and we call people. We pride ourselves on checking out everything. Several years ago, Harriet Adams (Stratemeyer's daughter) was looking for material for a Nancy Drew book she'd titled *Secret of the Forgotten City*. I happened to be in Las Vegas about that time and heard someone mention a lost city. There really *is* a lost city out there. Part of it is buried under Lake Mead. So Mrs. Adams and I went back to Nevada and spent several days with the head of a museum there. I tape-recorded everything he told us — and all of that was helpful in the writing of that Nancy Drew book."

Bats? Lost cities? No wonder Nancy Drew and The Hardy Boys were naturals for TV.

"All the Spooky Things"

Nancy Drew and The Hardy Boys came on television at a time when there was growing demand for shows that were non-violent. "I think that's why we finally got the shows on the air," said producer Joyce Brotman. "The people who write the books insisted that the TV material be non-violent. We agreed."

So did many people in the television industry. People everywhere had been studying the effects of TV violence on viewers. They hadn't agreed on much. At times they couldn't even agree on what they meant by violence. If Marie Osmond hits Donny in a comedy sketch, is that an act of violence? Some said yes, others said no.

But the battle cry had been sounded. And it was heard by TV networks and producers

The Hardy Boys are on to something! They've found a clue in the laboratory that may break their case wide open. These young actors have helped turn a series of popular books into an exciting TV series.

alike. There were increasing signs that viewers did, indeed, want shows that were less brutal and more fun. NBC tried out a show called *The Life and Times of Grizzly Adams*. The stars were a great big bear and a man who loved all animals. The show was a hit.

Nancy Drew and The Hardy Boys came on the scene in the middle of the TV season. Most midseason replacements don't make it. Shows already on the air have too big a head start. The young detectives didn't start strongly but they became increasingly popular with young viewers. And nobody could forget that it was young people who kept *Happy Days* alive while it was struggling to find itself. *Happy Days* went on to become the #1 show on TV. Could

Nancy Drew and The Hardy Boys do the same?

They started with one tremendous advantage. They did not have to be introduced to the viewers. TV reaches a huge audience. But so had Nancy Drew and The Hardy Boys in their long careers as amateur detectives. They were, in fact, older than the medium itself.

"Their books have sold consistently well over the years," Nancy Axelrad said. "But since the TV show appeared, sales have practically doubled!"

Glen Larson, the executive producer of the TV series, is a veteran television producer. "And what a talent he is!" exclaimed Joyce Brotman, one of the show's two producers. "Glen wrote the scripts for the first shows of both Nancy Drew and The Hardy Boys. He directed the first Hardy Boys, and he wrote the theme music. He's an amazing man." And he should know what young people like, she might have added. He has six children.

"We all learned so much the first season," Joyce said. "This was the first show Arlene Sidaris and I ever produced. She handled Nancy Drew; I handled The Hardy Boys. But we both went to the 'dailies' of the two shows. That's when you look at the film that was shot the day before. You must look at it as soon as it's developed to see what you have. If any changes are to be made, they must be made immediately. Otherwise the actors, the sets, the costumes, and so on may change — and you can't afford to go backward!"

After the filming is finished, an editor puts it all together and begins the process of cutting it down to fit the time allowed. "We look at it four or five times while that's being done," Joyce explained. "Then we bring the actors in to 'loop.' That means they redo any lines you can't hear. If the filming was being done outside, you might hear a car horn that you have to get rid of, or you might not be able to hear the voices. Outside scenes are generally looped as a matter of course. Inside scenes — or interiors — are looped when necessary. There are other times when looping is necessary. For example: If we're shooting in a place where we can't fit the big camera, we use a smaller one. It's noisy, and we may end up with camera noises on the film

"All of that," Joyce added, "is production work that goes into a film before its gets to TV. All of that takes time — and that's what we didn't have when the series first began."

They got their time, however. ABC cancelled some of its shows that spring. But they stuck by Nancy Drew and The Hardy Boys. That gave the producers, writers — and everybody else involved with the show — time to figure out what they wanted to do with these three young people.

"We did not insist that the TV shows be drawn from the stories." Nancy Axelrad said. "What we wanted them to do was draw on elements from the books: the tunnels, caves, all the spooky things."

Spooky things! That's what readers of Nancy Drew and The Hardy Boys have come to expect. Millions of us grew up chilling to their every adventure. We *want* dark, spooky nights and wind howling through the trees overhead. We want Nancy Drew and The Hardy Boys out there prowling around in the dark tracking down criminals.

The tunnels, the watery caves, the blinking lights — we read and shiver. Nancy Drew is tied up in an attic with a black widow spider on the loose! How can we possibly leave her there while we go to eat our dinners? Usually, we can't. And we don't.

It's great fun to see Nancy Drew and The Hardy Boys on the TV screen. But whatever happens to them on television, one thing is certain. For all of us who read their books, they don't really live on TV. They live in that most important place of all — our own minds and imaginations.